Tracking the Strategic Plan

by Rochelle O'Connor
Senior Research Associate

A Research Report from The Conference Board

Ministry of Education, Ontario
Information Centre, 14th Floor,
Mowat Block, Queen's Park,
Toronto, Ont.   M7A 1L2

658
.4012
O 18t

Contents

	Page
WHY THIS REPORT	iv
1. THE CONTEXT FOR TRACKING STRATEGY	1
2. COMPANY MONITORING PRACTICES	4
Formal and Informal Approaches	4
The Monitoring Process	6
The Focus of Strategic Review	6
3. SIGNIFICANT ISSUES IN MONITORING	10
Measurement and Performance	10
Linking Operating and Strategic Plans	11
Other Major Concerns	15

Exhibits

1. Instructions for Strategic Program Review—An Industrial Products Manufacturer	7
2. Business Plan Format to Indicate Shifts in Position—A Chemical Company	8
3. Guide for Strategic Business Units to Measure Strategy Performance—A Diversified Manufacturer	13

Why This Report

Over the past decade, corporate planners from major companies have focused on the development and refinement of more effective planning processes, an activity in which The Conference Board has participated in its research and conference programs. The assumption behind all this effort was that better planning would lead to better plans.

It was not a bad assumption as far as it went. But given the uncertainties of competition and of the external political and social forces with which companies must contend, it was only a matter of time before widespread disenchantment would arise over the practicality and realism of plans. That disenchantment has come with a vengeance, and with it increased interest in the means by which the fulfillment of strategic plans can be measured.

This report, the sixth in a series of biannual surveys of the Board's Panel of Planning Executives, examines the approaches their companies make to achieve management control of the plan. It also deals with the problems and issues these planners encounter when they attempt to track the plan. The Conference Board is grateful to the 67 planners who shared their experiences in making this report possible.

JAMES T. MILLS
President

Chapter 1
The Context for Tracking Strategy

Is THE COMPANY moving in the right direction?

Are its strategies correct?

Are they being executed as expected? If not, why? And what should be done?

These questions form the framework of one of the basic concerns of management. For top management, the ability to monitor progress toward goals of long term and major consequence speak to the viability and worth not only of the planning exercise, but of the entire managerial enterprise. For the corporate planner, whose responsibility it is to preside over a companywide planning process, the issues of monitoring the plan and assessing the adequacy of the process are integral to the planning process itself.

Tracking strategy, or evaluating progress toward a predetermined objective, has become a more important issue in recent years for several reasons. The most obvious is purely procedural: The development of formal strategic planning systems, a process still evolving in many firms, raises questions of operational and strategic control. In the initial years, of course, most company planning systems focus on developing planning as a discipline for managers to help run their businesses. The emphasis is on familiarizing managers with the idea of planning and with developing a planning system that they will accept. All this stress on getting managers to plan has often deferred and even obscured the ultimate goal of a doable strategic plan with achievable objectives. But that stage has now come for many organizations: a time to see the results of strategies painstakingly wrought, and to be able to measure them credibly.

Even where formal planning systems do not exist, the recent volatility of the economic, political, social and technological environment within which companies now operate has led many top managers to question both the definition and conduct of their major businesses. For such managers, strategic review is seen as increasingly important.

Despite the heightened interest in monitoring the implementation of strategy, literature on the subject is sparse and indications are that new methods and techniques for gauging strategic progress have not yet entered management systems and procedures.[1]

Thus, the subject of this sixth survey of The Conference Board's Panel of Planning Executives concerns company efforts to track the progress of the strategic plan and the achievement of strategic objectives. The panel members were asked to describe their company's monitoring process, the focus of the effort as it related to performance and measurement, the basic differences in approach to tracking strategic performance and operational plans, and what improvements they would like to see in their procedures.

The survey findings show that what the participating planners have in mind when they speak of "tracking the strategy" is a range of strategic approaches monitored at different levels in the corporation by a variety of formal and informal management systems. This wealth of perspectives nevertheless points to several basic conclusions:

The plans that are monitored are primarily the strategic and operating plans of individual profit centers, divisions or other units of the organization.

Consequently, the responsibility for monitoring these plans and checking on strategic progress falls to the manager of the unit involved, the executive who bears the responsibility for developing and carrying out the plan.

"Our whole approach to planning and measurement has been to help the individual managers employ a planning methodology in a manner that strengthens the

---

[1] See, for example, J. H. Horovitz, "Strategic Control: A New Task for Top Management," *Long Range Planning,* June, 1979; Charles H. Roush, Jr. and Ben C. Ball, Jr., "Controlling the Implementation of Strategy," *Managerial Planning,* November-December, 1980; and Waldron Berry, "Beyond Strategic Planning," *Managerial Planning,* March-April, 1981.

overall management of the business. It is they who have the greatest need to document strategies and monitor progress against key milestones," according to a diversified company's planning vice president.

Top corporate managements may monitor strategies on a regular basis, or they may satisfy themselves with irregular reviews of varying depth and thoroughness. But except in single-business companies—where top management has the primary responsibility for business strategy and does not delegate it to the heads of lower divisions or subsidiaries—the focus of top-management monitoring efforts is on the companywide, rather than business, strategy. The field of view is broader, usually encompassing several businesses and the future of the company as a whole.

In its monitoring efforts, top management is primarily concerned that the business planning effort of the individual profit centers is being effectively carried out. Long-range profit performance of individual units is most important as it bears on the profit performance of the company as a whole.

A food company's planning director explains: "We run a form of 'quality control' check on our strategic plan numbers against actual results—specifically on the earnings per share projections that are a result of the total plan. This is done at the corporate level in order that we can track any evidence of our plan becoming 'blue sky'— not related to reality."

Further, in most of the companies represented in the survey, even among those that take the matter most seriously, monitoring strategy is as yet a relatively informal affair compared with the typically more structured operational plan-review process.

The 67 responses to the survey suggest that tracking the strategy is a difficult and sophisticated process requiring considerable thought and care. Traditional review procedures, for example, do not always adequately point up progress—or lack of it—toward qualitative goals. The thinking behind establishing strategic review systems is shared by the planning vice president of a large diversified manufacturer:

"While many businesses over the past few years have made great progress in the art of developing, articulating and communicating their strategies, few have made progress in the art of explicitly reviewing these strategies logically, consistently and effectively. In fact, one of the major problems facing corporation managers in this age is the difficulty of integrating increasingly good and creative strategic thinking into the day-to-day management of the corporation and its businesses.

"The inability to track performance against strategy effectively is, we believe, one of the main causes of this difficulty. A more and more common complaint is: 'I'm sure we've got a great strategy, but how can we be sure that it is working?'

"Part of the problem is that, over their histories, all corporations have developed systems for tracking short-term operating and financial performance that serve their somewhat limited and short-term purposes well, but that rarely serve as an effective means for tracking strategic performance. Also, in addition to traditional financial information, there are masses of data available to the business manager from various sources, but there are no formal means for identifying and measuring those key variables that reflect the driving forces of the business."

The time span necessary to gauge a long-term strategy adequately is another dimension that must be factored into the monitoring procedure, according to an industrial steel products planner:

"The strategic plan should be a long-range directional program that provides a cohesive plan within which the operating unit makes current decisions. Measuring such a plan must then take place over some relatively long period of time rather than the conventional month, quarter, or even one-year period. Having made the point that measurement must be over some relatively long-time period, the additional point must be made that management needs some indication of current progress toward the attainment of long-range goals."

These are basic issues that have to be addressed when considering the elements of a strategic plan-monitoring system. Additional concerns are the nature of strategic planning itself, and the need to encourage creativity and initiative in managers.

The planning executive of a diversified food and restaurant firm comments:

"We have attempted to make a separation between long-range planning and strategic planning. Long-range planning is a continuous, trend-oriented extrapolation of the recent past, and contains a substantial amount of quantification. Strategic planning is discontinuous and leaps ahead to envision competitive developments and environmental impacts at some point in the future. Long-range planning is used as a control technique and is monitored; strategic planning seeks creative responses in an anticipatory setting that does not lend itself to elaborate monitoring."

Two respondents carry this point even further and offer these views:

"There is an inherent trade-off in a formal planning process between explicit requirements for detail, and the freedom allowed to the general manager to use maximum creativity in tailoring his plan to the unique requirements of the industry. We tend to lean toward the free expression side of this choice. As a result, incomplete as our tracking program may seem from a formal basis, we feel that it provides maximum freedom to run the business for both the business unit general manager and the group executive."

—an electrical products manufacturer

* * *

"I don't really see the strategic plan as a formal tracking plan. It should be of such a nature that it will encourage broad and creative thinking about a business and its future course, and yet still be dimensionally sound to the extent that it needs to be a reasonably meaningful guide for capital requirements. I don't think we should create an inhibiting climate with the managers by saying, in effect: 'You are going to be carefully tracked and measured against this plan.' At the same time, however, by including reference and comparisons in operating reviews we can raise the level of consciousness of a 'realistic strategic plan' so that we will not be seeing a series of 'wait until next year' plans which are never really achieved. There should be a logical continuity in the plans through this cross-referenced process."

— a food products company

What role does the corporate planning executive have in the monitoring and control aspects of the planning process for which he or she is responsible? In the large majority of the companies participating in the survey, the planning unit has no direct involvement with the monitoring process.

Indirectly, a number of planning executives believe, their responsibilities for the planning function bear considerably on the evaluation of plan progress. For example, by designing a process that guides the identification of issues, development of objectives, and selection of strategies, they are providing the framework for intelligent assessment of the plan. Further, in the role as directors of the planning function, they act as catalyst, coordinator, data gatherer, and support for senior management—activities that they feel provide insight into plans and develop a basis for challenging and judging real progress. In other words, by planning the planning system, they also design the process of control.

In four of the participating companies—all coincidentally nonmanufacturing companies—the corporate planning officer is charged with following up major variances that show up in reviews. An insurance company planning director (with other accounting responsibilities) states: "The role of the planning officer is to evaluate current progress toward planned objectives and to coordinate any unplanned and expedient actions. In addition, through the role as budgeting officer, all new unbudgeted projects and major variances from planned expenditures, either over or under budgets, come to the attention of the planning officer for review and coordination."

A few other respondents report varying degrees of monitoring responsibilities:

"Progress is monitored and reported quarterly. Responsibility for the basic monitoring effort has been given to the corporate planning and analysis staff, one of several corporate staff groups involved in the operational and strategic planning process."

— a chemical company

* * *

"The achievement of corporate long-term goals consists of attaining the individual company goals and the achievement of diversification activities, carried forth by the corporate strategic planning organization. An assessment of these individual elements is performed annually by the corporate strategic planning organization and presented to corporate senior management."

— an aircraft and defense products firm

What Kind of Monitoring System?

Recognizing the constraints and trade-offs that must be considered in any process that monitors strategy, a business forms company's planning director observes: "The question is: What system is most compatible with the culture, does not represent a burden, and delivers the key signal that follow-up is every bit as important as the plan itself?"

Chapter 2
Company Monitoring Practices

OF THE 67 planning executives participating in this survey, 51 say that their companies in some way monitor the progress being made toward the achievement of strategic objectives. They accomplish this through both formal strategic-monitoring processes and through less systematized review procedures. For both of these systems, the focus of the review is the attainment of goals set forth in the strategies adopted by the units.

Formal and Informal Approaches

In a formal, structured strategic-monitoring system, reported by 30 of the companies, there is generally a prescribed format for reporting on strategic progress. In these cases, the review is frequently designed into the strategic planning process itself, through milestones, reporting dates, and measurement criteria.

The less formalized systems of the other 21 companies usually address the same types of issues and the same kinds of measurements that distinguish strategic review from operating results. The difference between formal and informal tracking systems, for example, is frequently in the eye of the beholder, rather than in the substance of the review. Many of the participating survey executives balk at identifying their monitoring procedures as "formal" systems, yet they describe the same kinds of measures and strategic focus as others who claim a formal tracking system.

For example, a steel company's planning director explains:

"In the strictest sense, we do not have a formal system for monitoring the strategic plan. Having said that, however, I want to point out that: (1) We do monitor elements of the plan; (2) We prepare a plan each year in which we identify and evaluate key issues, assumptions, environments, and so on, and contrast them with past positions; and (3) We attempt to link (although not well) the one-year plan (program of operations) with the strategic plan and monitor the one-year plan.

"In the broader sense, therefore, we do the following in tracking for strategic planning:

"(a) Monitor the economic and steel environment and describe changes that are perceived to be occurring in the market against the plan outlook.

"(b) Track annually issue identification and assumption review. Key issues and assumptions are tracked on a year-by-year basis to develop consistency and to highlight changes that appear to be happening either in terms of the issues or the assumptions.

"(c) Since steel is capital intensive, we monitor capital-spending projections and attempt to identify and track major replacement and pollution- abatement projects envisioned in the plan.

"(d) We monitor cash-flow performance to ensure that we have the financial resources to carry out the capital program incorporated in the plan.

"(e) Periodically (once every few years) we monitor specific measurement of performance against past plans. These measures include such items as steel shipments, margins and net income."

The vice president of corporate development in a retail chain also says that his company does not have a formal system for monitoring the strategic plan, but nevertheless maintains a strategic perspective:

"Monitoring takes place informally in three ways:
• "Regular status meetings between operating company CEO's and the corporate line executive to whom they report;
• "Review of capital-project requests and long-range financial goals from a strategic perspective;
• "Review of progress against the previous strategic plan, as appropriate, in the following year's strategic planning meeting.

"The fundamental reason for this is that we do not treat strategic planning as a stand-alone management system. Rather, it is integrated with our other corporate management systems as both user and provider and information and direction. Because of this integrated understanding of our management process, we anticipate that the primary results of strategic plans will be manifested in other management systems and are best monitored as part of those systems."

There are, in addition, companies whose planning and monitoring systems differ at their various organizational levels, with correspondingly different degrees of formality. In one such case, the monitoring process looks like this:

"The only formal reviews against the long-term strategic objectives are those contained in the strategic plan itself and those that occur in the short-term plan. Informal monitoring is quite often done at the operating unit level when there are significant variances from the current growth path. The formal process involves the corporate planning unit, corporate operating executives, and group operating executives, in addition to operating unit personnel that are affected. The informal monitoring process is primarily within the operating unit management and, to a lesser extent, involves group management. The corporate planning department is deeply involved in the formal process, but does not necessarily participate in the informal process."

The planner in a large oil company states that in his firm strategic planning is considered "as three interrelated activities: a long-range plan, a near-term (annual) plan, and strategic issue or major project reviews." A corollary to this situation is manifested by several survey participants who say that there are no strategic plans in their companies. Although planning is done, it may be solely operational planning with some strategic implications, or plans with undefined objectives, or evolving planning systems that have not yet produced plans that can be monitored. Nevertheless, a number of these companies do review, in some manner, the progress and results of whatever plans they do develop.

The planning executive of an industrial products manufacturer says that while his firm does not have an acknowledged system for monitoring the long-range plan, this, "in one sense, conforms to our management strategy of competitive reaction to customer and market cycles. This approach is supported by an industry neither limited by capital or lengthy capital equipment procurement constraints. For these reasons, a two-year plan with a detailed rolling twelve-month budget (total is three years) receives maximum attention and measurement. In contrast, the strategic or long-range plan format's purpose is to outline and define areas of development, proposed business directions, and preliminary financial forecast as a road map for the future."

In a natural resources company, the planning director interprets the practice in his organization thus: "Although included as an integral part of the planning process in policies and procedures statements and planning flow diagrams, in actuality we have never formally monitored progress of the strategic plan or the achievement of strategic objectives. Each year the planning staffs have been directed to prepare a new, improved strategic plan to restart the process. We have thus only monitored the first year of each annually prepared plan."

Clearly, most organizations have developed ways of monitoring that do not necessarily fit rigid categorization. This is particularly apparent where the review of strategic performance is tied in to a variety of management systems. Several participating planners note such cases in their firms. An example of a multifaceted monitoring process is described by the strategic planning director of a chemical company:

"The management-by-objectives system for individuals is utilized in varying degrees throughout the organization as a monitoring and control system for strategic objectives. The system which we use is called "Management by Results" (MBR) and requires a statement of three- to five-year (i.e., longer term) results expected. Hence, it lends itself to monitoring and control of strategic objectives, and provides a ready mechanism for linking strategic business objectives with shorter range goals for individual employees. The corporate planning unit participates in the MBR program; however, insofar as the business strategy objectives are concerned, its role is simply to ensure that strategic objectives are made explicit so that they *can* be utilized in a system administered by line management assisted, in general, by the human resource management function in the corporation.

"We also employ a form of zero-based budgeting—titled "Priority Resource Budgeting" (PRB)—that provides a ready method for associating short-term (annual) resource allocations with the achievement of longer term strategic objectives. As is the case with MBR, corporate plans department utilizes the PRB process, but only for its own activities. The controller function manages the PRB effort and the planning function responsibility is to ensure that the strategic objectives are clarified and sufficiently visible so as to provide the necessary orientation to the budgeting process.

"As illustrated by the MBR and PRB activities mentioned above, the activities on monitoring progress toward strategic objectives, which are formally conducted at the corporate level, represent only a small part of the monitoring and control process conducted within the corporation. Over and above the systems mentioned, there are very important tactical planning and tactical-plan monitoring activities conducted at many operating levels throughout the corporation. These must all be focused so as to be consistent with the strategy criteria defined as a part of the corporate consensus on the strategy for the strategic planning unit, made explicit in the business direction paper and reinforced by expression in both plans and specific resource-allocation requests reviewed at the corporate level.

"Our total management system is built on a basis of being 'driven' by the corporate consensus on business strategy."

The Monitoring Process

Reviews of strategic performance, whether formal or as part of an informal process, cover different time frames and are scheduled accordingly during the year in the surveyed companies. Although in some companies evaluation reviews are on a more or less stand-alone basis, it is much more common for them to take place in conjunction with other planning or control activities.

The most frequently reported strategy review takes place annually, usually when plans are developed or updated. Twenty-one companies say that they assess strategy at that time.

As the planning cycle gets under way, there is a general appraisal of performance during the previous year against the strategic plan—its goals, financial objectives and programs. When new plans are presented for approval, senior management generally measures the advance toward objectives. A food company executive says: "The annual development of the new three-year plan, and its subsequent review, provides for a progressive review and affirmation of strategic objectives for the operating units." And an insurance company planner asserts: "The approval process for short-term operational plans and budgets is itself a monitoring device to relate these plans to long-range objectives. Substantial effort is made in this process to determine that short-range plans are at least not incompatible with objectives."

In a number of firms, planning procedures ask for comparison between current and previous plans. (One diversified manufacturer requires a comparison between the current plan and the previous plans for the past four years.)

On a broad scale, however, this could prove a mighty undertaking and several planners specifically note that they usually only ask for limited comparisons between prior and current years, focusing only on a few selected areas of interest. The planning director of an information services company says: "Constantly comparing current plans with previous plans can be cumbersome and not very productive. We ask for explanations of differences only on a rifle-shot basis, where top management or (the corporate planning unit) feel explanations are needed."

Fifteen companies in the survey track the progress of strategy at regularly scheduled operating plan reviews, usually quarterly but often even more frequently scheduled. The one-year operating plan is considered a milestone of the longer term strategic plan in many companies; thus, the milestones of the operating plan are reasoned to be assessment points for the long-term plan as well.

Other companies in the survey report that they review progress toward strategic objectives two or three times a year. And some tracking efforts involve specific types of review. The planning director of a technology company, for instance, says that in his firm, "Upper management reports are generated on a quarterly basis, but the central strategic tracking system also incorporates 'exception' reports that are generated as significant events are detected by the individual program managers and input to the system. These exception reports may be either positive or negative, that is, a major failure, a danger sign, or a substantial achievement such as a technological breakthrough."

Still other companies report that they may have informal reviews irregularly, or on an ad hoc basis, depending on the need perceived. These frequently relate to particular strategies under way that require close scrutiny, or major investment projects. Although 13 companies in the survey say they have no tracking procedures for the strategic plan, several mention that it is not uncommon to look at the progress of strategies during annual or quarterly plan reviews.

The Focus of Strategic Review

Monitoring the progress and results of plans is management's primary method of exercising strategic control. Yet several of the surveyed participants stress a distinction between the monitoring effort that seeks simply to see how well things are going, and the higher level of effort needed for providing organized feedback to direct and correct strategy. In the latter type of monitoring, which aims at identifying problems and pointing toward corrective action, the selection of targets for review is often based on critical issues. The focus is usually on major programs and on specifically chosen businesses.

According to the planner of a forest products company: "More frequent special reviews relating to strategic performance are usually triggered when we follow up on the progress of a major expansion or start-up of a facility, or when major changes take place in our marketing thrust by specific geographic or major customer group."

Selected programs are also the focus of review in the context of strategies for the business in a diversified manufacturing firm: "The strategic plan-monitoring process focuses on the status of action programs that support plan strategies. When strategic plans are submitted, a summary of action programs is provided. The company's quarterly operations-review process includes a presentation on progress on major action programs [Exhibit 1].

Exhibit 1: Instructions for Strategic Program Review—An Industrial Products Manufacturer

---

1982 First Quarter Operations Review

General

1. The intent of this portion of the quarterly operations review is to provide a brief status report on the group's major strategic programs.

2. The strategic program review should be limited to the group's top five priority programs. The attached form is to be completed for each program and submitted with the financial portion of the operations review package. This form can be utilized as an overhead viewgraph if desired. It is recommended, however, that overhead slides which highlight only the most important discussion items be prepared for presentation to the chairman's office.

3. Corporate Planning and Development will provide group presidents with a list of suggested programs by March 31, based on the 1982 operating plan and last year's strategic plan.

Form Requirements

1. Provide a brief two- or three-line description highlighting the critical elements of the program.

2. Under the heading "Key Action Items," list the major action components that comprise the strategic program. While main emphasis should be placed on action items to be completed in 1982, longer range action items should also be indicated. In all cases, the final action item indicating program completion should be shown.

3. Under the heading "Original Completion Date," indicate the month and year in which each key action item of the program was to be completed as envisioned in the 1982 operating plan and/or the 1981 to 1985 strategic plan.

4. The "Current Completion Date" should provide an update to currently anticipated month and year of completion of each action item.

5. Under the heading "Responsibility," show the function and/or individual with principal responsibility for completing each phase of the program.

6. Under the title "Commentary on Program Status," the following should be provided:

    a. A brief restatement of the broad objectives of the program. Highlight any significant change in objectives since the inception of the program.

    b. Discuss the impact of any changes in external environment or competitive action on the success of the program.

    c. Review the progress of the program and indicate major reasons for any program slippage. Discuss anticipated future changes in program timephasing shown on the form.

    d. Discuss your recommendations as to whether the program should be (1) continued as originally planned, (2) accelerated, (3) redirected, (4) deemphasized, or (5) discontinued. If a change is indicated, provide appropriate supporting commentary.

The only quantitative measurement at this juncture is the completion date of each key action item within the strategic program."

In a firm that reviews the strategic performance of its units through several different management procedures, "an important corporate-level review is conducted by the Executive Management Committee (EMC)—the top five executives in the corporation plus the vice president of corporate plans and business development as secretary," the planning director states. "These reviews are named 'Strategy Criteria Progress Reviews,' and the progress of 10 to 12 businesses per year are reviewed by the top management responsible for these businesses. The 10 to 12 businesses per year (out of a total of approximately 40 in the corporation) are selected by the EMC on the basis of leverage on corporate performance in the near to long term, recent anticipated external or internal changes, and so on."

The selection of critical factors for review presents a challenge for management. While internal performance measures are the almost universal starting point, some companies try to look beyond the usual financial measures to gain a more externally oriented view of how the firm is positioned. A chemical company's vice president of planning explains:

"The focus in our strategic plan-tracking effort is on *trends*. These include such factors as market growth rate, capacity utilization, addition of new capacities, market share of ourselves and our competitors, and general profit levels in the industry. These include latest forecast, but also show changes from the prior year. [Exhibit 2] represents our strategic data base, which is updated on an

Exhibit 2: Business Plan Format to Indicate Shifts in Position—A Chemical Company

LONG-RANGE PLAN
BUSINESS UNIT SUMMARY
(IN MILLIONS)

DIV./SUB _____
BUSINESS UNIT _____

STRATEGIC CLASSIFICATION _____

ACTUAL   FORECAST

19__ 19__ 19__ 19__ 19__ CUM 19__ 19__ 19__ 19__ 19__ CUM 19__

U.S. Consumption-Units
Five-Year Growth Rate—%

Industry Capacity:
  Nameplate
  Utilization—%

Market Share—%
Relative Market Share—%

Market Position

(Co.) Sales—Units
Five-Year Growth Rate

(Co.) Capacity:
  Nameplate
  Utilization—%

Unit Price

(Co.) Net Sales
Five-Year Growth Rate—%
% Resale

Adjusted Gross Profit—%

Operating Expenses—%

Earn. Before Int. & Taxes
Adjustments-Leased Assets
   Adj. Earn. Before Int. & Taxes

Earnings From Operations
Earnings From Operations—%

Capital Employed
Return on Capital Employed
Five-Year Average—%

Capital Expenditures

Net Cash Flow

○ Corresponding data from last year's plan

□ Current five-year compounded growth or annual average

8   TRACKING THE STRATEGIC PLAN

annual basis. For instance, in the squares we show this year's compounded growth rate for five years, and in the circles the ones presented a year ago. This will tell us not only shifts in past as against future trends, but also changes in assumed trends from one plan to another. In other words, it tells management at a glance what the particular shifts are in that specific business unit.

"Some of the things we discuss at that time are, for instance, whether we want to gain market share or hold it. This, in turn, will have implications on other strategies. However, once such a decision is made it will be monitored and reviewed at least on an annual basis."

The vulnerability of certain industries to the economy, market conditions, and business cycles plays a large part in the way they structure their planning process and in what and how they monitor.

In this survey, for example, the steel, oil and chemical company spokesmen, in particular, allude to their watch on the external environmental factors that significantly affect the execution of strategies. Monitoring those indicators critical to their operations, they believe, is needed to provide a better perspective for strategic evaluation. (A large chemical company, for example, has recently installed a system that tracks prices and current cost items on a monthly basis.)

The planning vice president of a large consumer products company, on the other hand, states that the bulk of his company's business is relatively unaffected by the business cycle. "We keep our eyes glued to market-share trends and to maintaining the vitality of our brands as long-range propositions."

For many of the survey participants, the focus of strategic review appears to be based on what can be readily assessed. The difficulties of evaluating qualitative goals and targets, for example, have resulted in the monitoring of those elements that are more easily measurable and that are supported, for the most part, by the organization's accounting and management systems. The ease and comfort provided by readily captured numbers, for example, is emphasized by the planning executive of a glass products manufacturing firm, whose primary review during the year is on performance against budget rather than on performance against strategic plan. "Even at the annual strategic plan sessions," he states, "it is difficult to focus adequate attention on strategy rather than on numerical projections."

Focus on quantitative measures also can mean a focus on the near term, as explained by a chemical manufacturer's planning executive: "While we try to give the appropriate degree of emphasis to the measurement and tracking of long-term strategies, as a practical matter, we tend to focus more on short-term results and implications. One of the major reasons is the focus of U.S. public companies on short-term performance; however, a second, and equally valid, reason is that it is difficult to track results over a longer time period. Often, long-term results are obscured by changes in the environment, organization, objectives and other key variables."

A number of respondents indicate that their planning and control processes are budget-driven and operationally oriented, and that close monitoring of the first year of the plan is, in fact, a good indication of whether or not the course selected is being followed. A diversified metals and chemicals manufacturer states that: "The key checkpoint on progress has been the annual operating budget. This approach tracks progress on the first year's financial projections and action plans contained in the strategic plan document."

As might be expected, there is a good deal of emphasis on exception reports or variances from projected results. Even here, the attitudes of management can reflect broad or narrow biases. For an oil company planner:

"Plan monitoring should provide feedback to management on how a particular strategy is performing in the environment that actually evolves. Actual-to-plan variances have to be looked at in light of actual-to-assumed environmental conditions. Missing the plan is not necessarily bad; meeting the plan is not necessarily good. Plan monitoring assumes there will be variances; its purpose is to call management attention to possible needs, as well as opportunities, to make plan adjustments in a constantly changing world. Used this way, plan monitoring can help segregate uncontrollables from controllables, and contribute to a more rational management appraisal and reward system."

"It isn't necessarily 'bad' to depart from the strategic plan dimensions," a food products executive agrees, "but the rationale for changes (including any uncontrollable changes in the environment) is expected to be the subject for discussion."

Chapter 3
Significant Issues in Monitoring

TRACKING the strategic plan and the attainment of its objectives raises several important concerns for the respondents; many feel these have not been satisfactorily resolved. Techniques exist—or can be easily developed—for monitoring the operating plans and tactical action components of the strategic plan, for instance, but difficulties arise, in large part, because the shorter term elements do not always accurately measure the results achieved in the longer range plan. Thus, the significant issues that emerge in a monitoring process concern (1) valid measurements of performance that indicate long-term strategic results; and (2) the linkage between operational and strategic plans to ensure that they are compatible.

Measurement and Performance

At best, a periodic evaluation of strategic progress can only be a "stop-action" snapshot of a moving object against a changing background. Measuring current performance against long-range goals contains pitfalls, many planning authorities agree. They point out that quantitative criteria do not necessarily measure qualitative results. Stated differently, the numbers may be right, but not as the result of the execution of the desired strategy. For example, a company may be viewing an improved financial report that was achieved through a stringent cost-cutting program rather than the approved market-penetration strategy.

What kinds of measurements do the surveyed companies use to monitor the progress of the strategic plan? They are generally the common financial measures of performance and ratios that indicate growth and profit. They may vary somewhat among the participating companies, but they usually include revenues, sales, assets and other specific industry indicators, as well as market and competitive position.

Plan monitoring requires selecting the relevant "hard" numbers from a plan—income growth, cash flow, unit costs, market share, return on investment, and so on, and tracking performance against them. But in addition, advises one planning executive: "The 'hard' numbers need to be put in the right 'soft' perspective. As an example, if a plan calls for 10 percent per year income growth, it should also indicate whether this is meant to be more than, equal to, or less than industry performance. Then, sometime later, an actual growth of 8 percent can be looked at in light of both the 10 percent plan target and the actual industry experience of, say 7 percent, before strategic inferences are drawn. Strategic performance is essentially competitive performance. Attainment of strategic objectives should be looked at in a competitive light, not in terms of some absolute, and somewhat arbitrary, target pulled out of an historical plan."

Where major strategic change or risks are undertaken, one diversified manufacturer establishes formal milestones for such matters as market-share change, success in attracting distributors, product development, and major cost-improvement projects. For a forest products company, the focus of the measurement is variable and tends to be a function of what is contained in the strategy, but specific elements such as production as against design capacity, volume commitments to markets, product mix, and so forth, are frequently measured—often quarterly.

A technology firm monitors its strategic programs along four primary dimensions: customer satisfaction, innovation, productivity and human resources. "In each of these areas," the planning executive states: "The company has established a number of indicators of performance. In the customer-satisfaction area, it includes market share, product quality, delivery performance, and service. Innovation indicators are concerned with the flow of new products, the percentage of revenues they contribute, and an assessment of product performance relative to competition. Productivity measures cover both labor and capital productivity. Labor productivity focuses primarily on value added; capital productivity on various asset turnover ratios. In the human resources area, management is most concerned with assuring that critical positions in the company are filled with superior performers. Such measures operate at both corporate and division levels."

> **Strategic Performance Measurements**
>
> "(1) To be effective, strategic performance measures must be tailored to the particular strategy of each individual business unit. While there is a basket of generic strategic measurement tools, selection and application is highly dependent on detailed understanding of the particular business' strategy and situation.
>
> "(2) Strategic performance measurements have two dimensions:
>
> • *Monitoring key program implementation* to ensure that the necessary elements of strategy are being provided.
> • *Monitoring results* to ensure that the programs are having the desired effects.
>
> "(3) Strategy performance necessarily involves trade-offs—costs and benefits. Both must be recognized in any useful strategic performance measurement system:
>
> • *Objectives* assessing progress toward primary goals;
> • *Constraints* monitoring other dimensions of performance which may be sacrificed, to some degree and for some period, in order to achieve strategic objectives.
>
> "(4) Strategic performance measurements do not replace, but rather supplement, short-term financial measurements. They provide management with a view of long-term progress in contrast to short-term performance. They may indicate that fundamental objectives are being met in spite of short-term problems, and that strategic programs should be sustained despite adversity. They may also show that fundamentals are *not* being met although short-term performance is satisfactory, and, therefore, strategy needs to be changed.
>
> "(5) Strategic-performance measurement is linked to competitive analysis. Performance measurements should be stated in competitive terms (share, relative profitability, relative growth). While quantitative goals must be established, evaluating performance against them should include an assessment of what competition has been able to attain.
>
> "(6) Strategic-performance measurement is linked to environmental monitoring. Reasonable goals cannot always be met by dint of effort if the external world turns against us. Strategic-performance measurement systems must attempt to filter uncontrollable from controllable performance, and provide signals when the measures themselves may be the problem, rather than performance against them."
>
> —An oil company

A machinery manufacturer's planner believes that a most significant improvement in his company's tracking mechanism might come from the linkage of long-term performance to the achievement of long-term objectives, such as increased R&D, successful product development, and reversal of undesirable balance sheet problems.

For the most part, monitoring mechanisms such as performance and measurement criteria, and milestones, are built into the plan when it is submitted, rather than established separately, or later. An oil company executive explains this rationale: "We believe monitoring mechanisms have to be highly tailored to individual strategies and circumstances and, as such, should be an integral part of the plan itself."

Very few of the participating planning executives report that such measures are determined after the plan has been accepted. In a few cases, planners say that when it is not possible to define criteria with the proposed plan, they are established later.

A number of the responding executives are dissatisfied with the existing qualitative and quantitative measurements currently used in their companies. Even with the goals and milestones established in many planning systems, determining the progress of strategic programs is still very difficult. An oil company officer states: "We have not been completely satisfied with the current balance between quantitative forecasting and planning and more qualitative review of strategic issues. In this year's planning cycle, steps have been taken to improve on that balance in order to better focus management attention on key long-range issues. We do not feel that these changes will reduce our monitoring effort and that, in fact, they go hand-in-hand with an expanded use of milestones and target-return levels."

The kinds of improved measures being sought, among others, are principally in areas such as market share, relative cost position and profitability, technical leadership, and other indicators of competitive position. The link between financial performance and stock price is also being studied as a possible measure by a few participants. A defense industry firm's planning executive speculates that long-term monitoring parameters should be defined in terms that reflect the long-term objectives that are to be pursued. "How is the value of the organization reflected? Dividends are one way, but what is an indicator for future stock value?"

Linking Operating and Strategic Plans

Operating plans, the basic short-term elements of the long-term strategic plan, are reviewed and monitored regularly and frequently in most companies. According to many of the surveyed participants, the relatively short-term measurements of operating-plan performance and budget reviews are the criteria used in monitoring the

> **Measurements Should Reflect Strategic Trade-offs**
>
> "The items to be tracked in a plan-monitoring system must be customized to the unique characteristics of a particular business and its chosen strategy. It should focus on the key objectives of the business, and also reflect the trade-offs that may be required. As a simple example, a business whose strategy emphasizes increased market share should also monitor areas where sacrifices might have to be made (for instance, return on investment) to achieve the market-share objective. Similarly, the same business could choose a different strategy emphasizing improvement in return on investment. Here, share should also be monitored to track what might have to be given up to reach the profitability objective. In this simplified example, we have one business and two very different strategy options, although both have the same key measures. However, the measures would be interpreted very differently in the two cases. In the first, share is the objective; ROI is the constraint. In the second case, it is just the reverse.
>
> "Increasingly, we think of strategic measurements in terms of *paired objectives* and *constraints:* objectives to be maximized within constraints; constraints to be satisfied while pursuing objectives. This approach directly addresses the strategic trade-offs involved in a particular business, and allows them to be managed over time."
>
> —An oil company

progress of the strategic plan. This practice necessarily raises questions concerning short-term actions and long-range strategies, their linkage, and how the monitoring process may be involved.

Do the measures for one plan appropriately measure progress of the other? Are short-term results driving long-range strategy? Do needed or expedient changes in tactics affect the longer range strategy of the business? If so, where and how are these factors taken into account?

The potential conflict between short-term actions and long-range goals is real: "A company that reports no conflict between short-term and long-term simply is not facing any serious short-term problems at the time," declares one planning vice president. "This is not an 'either-or' choice," he adds. "Both are fundamentally important, and conflict between them is natural."

Nevertheless, this does not appear to be a problem to most of the respondents. They believe that balancing these two needs lies at the heart of the manager's job. A food company executive observes: "As long as the focus and direction of the business are understood—and they should be subject to change, should unforeseen or 'unplanned' events make that a desirable option—I don't see a dichotomy between current operational and long-term results. One of the purposes of a sound strategic plan and its observance within the corporate operating climate is to guard against expedient short-term actions that may violate the longer term view of the business. The purpose of the strategic plan," he adds, "is to provide perspective to what is currently being achieved and to assist in making decisions (and achieving results) consistent with the accepted longer term view of the operating business."

Nonetheless, a number of survey participants say that if short-term problems are severe, they frequently prevail over longer term considerations. Moreover, balancing the two perspectives can be made more difficult, some planners say, because of the way strategic plans are tracked.

> **Effective Performance Measurement**
>
> A broad strategic view prevails in a diversified manufacturing company whose planning vice president believes that to measure any strategy, "you must measure progress against the long-term goal of the strategy, as well as track the series of actions designed to achieve that goal." [See Exhibit 3.]
>
> He adds: "Some specific principles that we feel are important are:
>
> "1. Strategic-performance measurement should be both simple and sophisticated—sophisticated in that it correctly and comprehensively measures the essence of business performance and a business manager's execution of his strategy, yet simple enough so that the measures can be easily tracked, compiled and communicated.
>
> "2. A good 'system' will be natural, in that a good business manager will instinctively be measuring the most important variables already.
>
> "3. Both inputs (key actions and 'investments') and outputs (goals and performance) should be measured, and should be done so over time against important milestones.
>
> "4. A good measuring system will strengthen the strategy-development process as it will force managers to articulate their thrust, strategies, programs and action plans fully.
>
> "5. Both numbers (e.g., market share, return on sales) and words (e.g., design of product X completed) should be measured.
>
> "6. Strategy measurement 'systems' will draw upon—but be separate from—existing financial reporting systems, as they require broader sources of data and will reflect a considerable amount of selection, interpretation and assessment by the business manager.
>
> "7. Every strategy should be measured, not only the 'key' strategies.
>
> "8. Most strategies will be finite in time, and the measurement system should reflect this (i.e., track strategies against a beginning and an end).
>
> "9. Every strategy will likely have multiple rather than single measures. This search for a few indicators to measure or assess the essence of performance is key.
>
> "10. Measures should be flexible, changing as the dynamics of the business change."

Exhibit 3: Guide for Strategic Business Units to Measure Strategy Performance—A Diversified Manufacturer

The measurement of strategic performance must deal with a hierarchy ranging from the overall goals of the strategic thrust down to the key actions taken in support of programs relating to individual strategies. The hierarchy is diagrammed below:

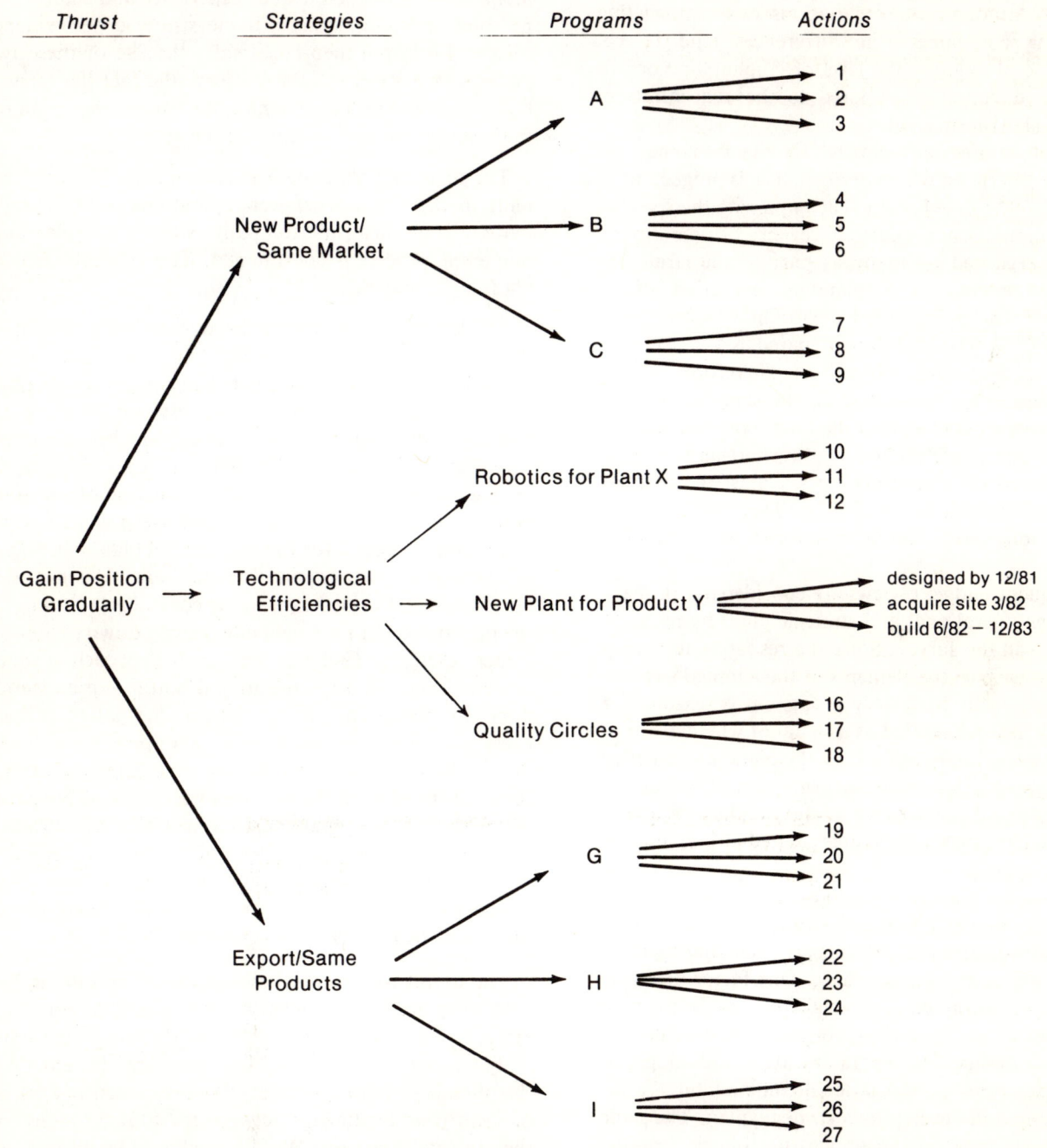

Measurement should be made at each level of the hierarchy, with both inputs and outputs measured as appropriate. It is not sufficient to measure only inputs (e.g., progress of the action plans against a time and budget schedule) or only outputs (e.g., the market share and financial goals implicit in the strategic thrust).

Whereas the shorter term plan is generally locked into a system of detailed reporting and tight budgetary controls, less formal, less quantitative evaluations govern strategic performance. Such a disparity necessarily complicates coordination.

How do the participants in this survey handle this? Most of the companies consider their system of operational performance reviews as the link to strategic-plan evaluation. Although many variations exist among the participating companies, the differences tend to be mainly those of degree—the level of emphasis accorded to strategic direction as opposed to the concentration focused on short-term results.

This is illustrated, principally, by the frequency of review, the criteria on which performance is judged, and, of course, on the time horizon encompassing the specific plan. The monthly and quarterly reviews of operational results are regarded by many as part of the strategic-monitoring process. The planning executive of a manufacturer of energy-related products says: "The company's short-term plans are prepared as a first step in meeting our long-range objectives. Therefore, at the product, market and project level, the short-term plans are compared in detail against the long-term plan and its objectives. One entire section of the short-term plan is then monitored on a monthly basis against the original plan—primarily on a financial basis. Therefore, in some sense, the long-term plan is monitored on a monthly basis."

The frequent budget reviews are considered a primary link between operational and strategic plans by many of the planners in the survey. Since the resources necessary to carry out each of the elements of the adopted strategy are allocated in the budgetary process, it is reasoned, a close watch here is justified as a signal of whether or not the plan is being implemented. As the planning executive of a large diversified manufacturing company puts it: "The primary linkage between strategy and operations is the specific treatment of resources aimed at building for the future."

Balancing the tightness or looseness of the linkage between operational plans and strategic plans requires delicate adjustments tailored to particular management systems, some respondents believe. One factor affecting the balance is the timing of strategic reviews. In the plan formulation stage of planning, for instance, the calendar is frequently designed to separate strategy and budget so that the exigencies of the latter do not inhibit the initiatives desired in developing a strategic plan. The same principle may apply in the timing of strategic reviews: When strategy is monitored together with operating performance, the tendency is to place major emphasis on current financial results, rather than on strategic objectives.

Not all share this view. The vice president of planning of a large diversified manufacturer describes the philosophy underlying a new program to monitor the progress of the strategic plan:

"We believe that the analysis of strategic performance should be done in parallel with the analysis of operating performance. This has two main purposes, one practical and one theoretical. From the practical side, this allows the systems currently in place, and with which the managers have a good deal of experience and comfort, to be used in conjunction with the strategic performance review. From the theoretical side, the use of these two systems in parallel should reinforce the fact that annual budgets should reflect, in detail, the current-year plan for the execution of the strategies of the business."

The corporate planning department is an active participant in the linkage between operational and strategic plans in a chemical company where the planning-budgeting process is coordinated. The vice president of planning comments:

"We have a very close link between the long-term plan and the operational plan. In fact, the first phases of the operational plan are coordinated in the corporate planning department. During this process, we set the goals and parameters for next year's operational plan and ensure that they are in line with our long-term strategic objectives. It also helps us to discuss allocation of resources before all the details of the budget are prepared. Only after the framework for the operational plan with regard to manpower, volume and financial objectives has been established is it turned over to the controller's section for the preparation of the final budget going down to the cost center level. We find this top-down approach is much more efficient than the traditional bottom-up budgeting done in many companies. Under the latter system, everybody first prepares a whole shopping list of items that add up to more than the total the company can afford. At the end, all the numbers have to be either pared down or changed completely to conform to their strategic objectives. Under our system allocation of resources takes place first, and we tell the operating divisions these are the parameters in which they can work. Based on this, they must then set their own priorities."

The degree of closeness, or separation, is another fact that needs resolution, according to several respondents. Here, again, the decision rests on the individual company's needs. In a bank holding company, for example, the planning executive states: "We are currently working on improving the linkage between the strategic plans and the budgetary process. We are working toward building action-plan tracking into the budgetary process so that it is not a separate, but rather an integrated, process."

The opposite is true for a chemical company that is "looking at ways to separate operational and strategic activities more clearly and intends to plan, budget and monitor these activities separately."

Clearly, these are decisions rooted in company experience and perceived needs. The shifts from tight to loose linkage, and vice versa, are determined as companies seek to improve their management and control procedures to respond to changing conditions. The planning director of an automotive products manufacturer describes his company's experience:

"Until now the company has operated its strategic and operational planning systems more or less separately. The operational plans, known within the company as the 'financial forecasts,' have been the principal tools for controlling the company's operations with a 12- to 18-month horizon in mind. The financial forecast and performance against it are reviewed three times per year at all levels of the corporation, and until now there has been little formal consideration of whether strategic goals are being achieved. The strategic planning cycle, done annually with a five-year horizon, has until now been kept quite separate from the financial forecast process. The thinking behind this was that this loose linkage made for freer, more creative strategic planning on the part of unit managers. That thinking has now changed. Starting this year, strategic plans are required to include implementation programs detailed with considerable specificity—milestones, capital expenditure requirements, strategic expense requirements, technology needs and so forth."

Several of the planning executives who responded disclaim any attempts to join the two evaluations. A pharmaceutical firm's planner asserts: "While the earlier planning efforts linked strategic and operational plans, we have 'disengaged' the two types of plans. The strategic planning effort now focuses on key issues and no effort is made to establish a linkage with operational plans except on a qualitative, judgmental basis."

In a company that manufactures engine parts, a separate procedure has also been set up for strategic assessment. Its planning executive says:

"Due to a relatively unique capability to develop capacity and react in the short term as an industry, we have set up a separate process by which to ensure a proper evaluation of long-range strategies. In particular, each year at least one or more complete strategic assessments, or reassessments, of specific existing or contemplated major activities are completed. These assessments are prepared and presented independently from the strategic plans. Individual assessments are also completed when an operating unit is confronted with an important strategic choice, having a significant impact on the future of the company. These independent assessments are eventually integrated with the plans and reviewed in subsequent years during the normal plan-review process. If deemed significant, these individual assessments are reviewed separately from the long-range plan for at least two to three years. Without these separate studies, the current tracking effort would not give adequate emphasis to long-term performance and results."

The linkage problem has been exacerbated in many companies by the stresses that economic conditions have placed on their planning procedures. The traditional measures of performance built into their plans, for example, no longer seem to offer a solid basis for evaluation. Developing other, more valid, standards may bring into question the possibility of bowing into a short-term perspective to the detriment of the longer term, more strategic overview. This predicament has been addressed in a steel company, whose planner explains:

"Up until a couple of years ago, projections in the strategic plan were made in constant dollars. Further, we did not attempt to predict the cycle in the first five years of the plan, even though we are in a very cyclical business. The belief was that this approach focused attention on long-term strategic direction. We have recently begun to put the cycle in the plan and have made projections in escalated dollars (in addition to constant dollars) to facilitate the monitoring process and to focus attention on linking the program of operations and the strategic plan. Our concern is that focus on linking may divert attention away from a long-term direction. However, short-term profitability is a key strategic issue in the steel business today."

Other Major Concerns

There are other specific problems and difficulties that concern many of the panel members responding to this survey. They perceive a need to improve not only elements of the monitoring system itself, but the planning process and other management systems that affect performance and motivation.

Forecasts and assumptions: Plans are formulated against assumptions of what conditions will be at some point in the future. But in a rapidly shifting environment, plans often have to be changed. Accomplishment, therefore, becomes relative, and established measures are not necessarily indicative of real progress toward strategic objectives.

Tracking and measurement are even more difficult when plans change from year to year, according to the planning director of a retail chain. "By the time one year's actual results are in, the plan has been revised," he observes. "Opportunity lies in focusing on those objectives and strategies that tend to remain stable even in periods of rapid change."

An oil executive comments that his industry has been through a period of extreme upheaval during the past decade, and strategic plans "are subject to rapid obsolescence. External changes may make a once reasonable strategic objective unattainable or irrelevant.

The major reason our company has not had a formal plan-monitoring system is that neither our plans nor their objectives have been durable enough to permit monitoring."

This points up a common complaint about inaccurate forecasts and assumptions, a situation that seems to bedevil a number of companies. A bank planner believes: "We could improve our tracking effort by monitoring the assumptions made when the plans are prepared against the actual environment in which they are carried out." And a forest products firm's planning executive believes that what needs improvement is "better sorting of critical errors in assumptions about macroeconomic and industry variables against management-controlled factors."

Here is how the planning director of a large chemical company views the problem:

"It would be desirable for our system to have greater focus on the measurement of factors external to the business but highly relevant to the business strategy. Most management systems for monitoring and control dwell too heavily on internal measurements readily available from accounting reports and/or necessitated by SEC reporting requirements. It is much more difficult to measure external elements, such as changes in competition and their strategies, sociopolitical, macroeconomic, geopolitical developments, and other similar factors. Hence, although they may often be the key leverage factors in a strategy, they are not always made explicit and monitored carefully enough to provide continuing verification of the viability of that strategy."

The reward system: The link between performance and compensation preoccupies several survey participants, who view this as a difficult and significant area for resolution. Some of the problems affect the plan-monitoring process. When compensation is directly tied to current financial results, managers are not likely to forgo these benefits for reward in a far distant future, and may regard tracking the long-term strategic objectives as threatening. In an oil company, for example, the close link between performance measurement and the reward system is considered an obstacle to implementing plan monitoring. "Especially in a business where the uncontrollables overwhelm the controllables, performance measurement is a sensitive subject. Nobody wants to be tied to a plan projection that looks out five years."

Linking managerial rewards to long-term performance has been an elusive goal for many companies. Several planners report that such programs are still evolving in their firms, and the problems are yet to be fully resolved. One approach is described by a transportation company's vice president of planning:

"We are looking at the possibility of using stock option incentives as a vehicle. This is longer term oriented—that is, what is being done today that should positively affect the long-term appreciation of the stock price. (Recognizing that some actions might have a negative impact on *short*-term profitability, it is better to keep the payoff in concert with the time frame of the longer term program benefits.")

Management commitment and time constraints: A number of respondents point out that their senior managements do not participate, or show sufficient involvement to make the tracking of strategic plans an undertaking of serious proportions. Other planners also report the absence of plan review at senior levels of the organization, thereby diluting the effectiveness of the monitoring process and, indubitably, the credibility of the planning effort.

Nevertheless, such demands on management, executives say, must be balanced with a consideration of their time constraints and the possible eruption of paper monsters. Thus, the planning executive of a computer manufacturing corporation cautions: "While improvement is always possible in a strategic-tracking system, the major danger is continuing to elaborate the system so that it becomes a major nonproductive 'drag' on the time and energy of the working-level strategic planners."

A textile company planner says: "The greatest improvements in our strategic planning-tracking process would come if corporate management and divisional management could meet periodically to review strategy. This would more clearly communicate corporate objectives to the divisions. Everyone would more likely be working toward the same goals."